Salt of the Earth

Doubts and Faith

Salt of the Earth

Doubts and Faith

Poems by

Patrick T. Reardon

© 2023 Patrick T. Reardon. All rights reserved.
This material may not be reproduced in any form, published,
reprinted, recorded, performed, broadcast,
rewritten or redistributed without
the explicit permission of Patrick T. Reardon.
All such actions are strictly prohibited by law.

Cover photo by Rembrandt, *The Return of the Prodigal Son*
on Wikipedia
Author photo by Patrick T. Reardon
Cover design by Shay Culligan

ISBN: 978-1-63980-412-2

Kelsay Books
502 South 1040 East, A-119
American Fork, Utah 84003
Kelsaybooks.com

For Mary Beth Zelasko and Eileen Novick
and
Sarah, John, Tara, David, Emmaline, Ulysses, Noah,
and, as always, Cathy.

Thanks to Thomas Pace and Renny Golden
and Haki Madhubuti and Joan Servatius.

Acknowledgments

Thanks to the publications where these poems first appeared, sometimes in somewhat different form:

After Hours: "The Archangel Michael"
All Shall Be Well: A Poetry Anthology for Julian of Norwich: "Fare Well"
America: "Corpus Christi Honeymoon"
Amethyst Review: "Canticle"
Bindweed: "Jesus Meets Little Sister Sandy's Mother"
Burningword Literary Journal: "Mercy! Charity! Faith! Holy!"
Calla Press: "Caress," "Holy Spirit," "John the Cousin," "The Good Shepherds"
Esthetic Apostle: "Pray"
Ground Fresh Thursday: "Blood and Flesh"
Jabber: "Song of the Swan"
Meat for Tea: "Poor Soul"
Outlaw Poetry: "Herod"
Pensive Journal: "Credo"
Poetry East: "Colonnade Saints"
Poetry Quarterly: "Red Beauty"
Pump Don't Work: "Visions"
Silver Birch: "Goddess," "I Want to Teach Emma Who Is Two"
Solum: "Adman Walked South"
Spank the Carp: "Soaked"
Time for Singing: "At the Hill Tomb," "Babylon Dream"
Tipton Poetry Review: "The Arc"
ucity review: "Lamentation"
Under a Warm Green Linden: "How puzzle the prayer"
Wild Roof: "Psalm Zero"
Write City Magazine: "Aaron," "Veronica"

Introductory Note

As this book's title and subtitle indicate, my experience of the spiritual dimension of life, the transcendent side, the divine aspect of every thing is a mix of belief and confusion. It is a recipe of glimpses and darknesses. Savor and pain are among the many threads in this fabric, a seamless garment. *Salt of the Earth: Doubts and Faith* is rooted in the Hebrew Bible and the New Testament, and many of the poems here are meditations on people and incidents in the Scripture. Others are ruminations on how, for instance, it would be if Jesus showed up at the front porch of a home in Chicago's Austin neighborhood, or how Mary might have acted in her grief, or what I might have to say to the statues along the colonnade at St. Peter's in Rome, or the ways in which my faith parallels that of Allen Ginsberg, or what would happen if the archangel Michael stopped into McDonald's for an Egg McMuffin, or what it might mean to honeymoon in Corpus Christi, Texas. Some of these poems are psalm-like prayers, and some are inspired by the Song of Songs. Others, such as "Credo" and "A New Year of Grace and Hope," are attempts to grapple with a great many complexities of living and believing and doubting. All of these are, in some way, visions, murky and ambiguous.

Patrick T. Reardon

Contents

Write the Vision

Mercy! Charity! Faith! Holy!	19
A New Year of Grace and Hope	20
Blood and Flesh	26
Credo	27
How Puzzle the Prayer	30
Magnifying the Lord	32
O Anointed One	37
Pilgrim	38
Foreheads Blazing	40
Psalm Zero	42
Lamentation	43
Pray, a Sequence	45
Alleluia	52

Look, I Am Sending You

The archangel Michael	55
Poor Soul	57
Prophet's Chair	59
An Act of God	60
Transfiguration mountain	61
Canticle	63
Holy Spirit	65
Sunlight on snow: a history	67
Jesus Meets Little Sister Sandy's Mother	68
Adman Walked South	69

The Bread Is Broken

Aaron	75
Visions	77
Voices	78

Red Sea	79
Babylon Dream	80
Testament, a Sequence	81
In Grief, Mary	87
Lowly	88
All Prophets Are Failures	89

The Boundless Perplexing Sea

Beatitude	93
Goddess	94
Hambone	96
Song of Songs, a Sequence	98
Corpus Christi Honeymoon	102
Fare Well	103
Colonnade Saints	106
Song of the swan	108
I Want to Teach Emma Who Is Two	109
Soaked	111

You are the salt of the earth. But if salt loses its taste, with what can it be seasoned? It is no longer good for anything but to be thrown out and trampled underfoot. You are the light of the world. A city set on a mountain cannot be hidden. Nor do they light a lamp and then put it under a bushel basket; it is set on a lampstand, where it gives light to all in the house.
—Matthew 5:13-15

Write the Vision

Mercy! Charity! Faith! Holy!

Holy the lone juggernaut! Holy the vast lamb of the middleclass!
Holy the crazy shepherds of rebellion!
—Allen Ginsberg, "Footnote to 'Howl'"

Answers are demanded of too many questions.

Write the vision, plain as a tabletop,
carved into barroom wood.

Vision has a time appointed,
presses on, will not lie. Wait for it.

Let go, ungrasp.
Let go, free.

Promissory note, hope.
The structure of bread.
A new moon over Highway 77.

Reptile, ogre, jackal, mud
—pure as any other thing.

Singer-king leapt and whirled
and claimed his loot, sinner
that he knew himself to be and prophet.

Wisdom is queen.

A New Year of Grace and Hope

And I saw a new year of grace and hope
in Alabama, Latvia and Laos,
now and at the hour with plague-song silenced,
with a feast of good letters,
with a cleansing in the nearest waters.
It never made the news.

And I heard: Here I am. Send me.

The punchline of each morning:
open-eye surprise,
putting one foot down and then the other,
jitterbug of breathing, moving.
Singing fools.

Before the Ark, I leapt in my cape,
in my ballet shoes, in my long-hair joy,
a lumbering buffoon, dancing bear,
fat organ-grinder monkey.

Listen to the coarse chorus
at their barred windows above us.
Hear the sky in the prison tune.
A denim holy day. Rough and rowdy praise.

Maranatha, maranatha, maranatha.

The prayer-wheel mutterings, rosary
labyrinths, steps counted—a rough
and seamless garment of rhythms
to wrap about the purple poor and
the owl-like hungry, the outcast soul and
the lost in a new year of grace and hope.

On the mountain side, I saw
fields of justice flourish,
fields of righteousness in morning sun,
lovingkindness in flower.

Stout semis murmured psalms on the Interstate,
canticles, sequences, alt rock hymns,
finger-snapping lullabies of Broadway.

    Let the infant calm the python.
    Let the baby, as a smooth stone, fly the arc of the sky.

    Let the child in golden robes and silver shoes
    tumble and somersault
    in the garden of rose-cheeked apples.

Two ways, the ancients taught, of life and of death.
Both meet.

Rejoice always. I say it again: rejoice.

        *

Blessed is the holy vine, the holy dog,
the holy concrete, the name that is
revered, the night ghosts, the soiled bed,
pustules and pimples, nervous tics,
the lexicon of the lost, the angels
rollerskating down Clark Street, the
McDonald's wrapper scripture skittering
here to there curbside, a silent Ecclesiastes,
an assault on stone gods.

Breath. Mere breath. Breath!

Sand-paint the sacred space
in a new year of grace and hope.
Finger open the crack in the cosmos curtain.
Stones and dead bones blooming,
petroglyphs and pictographs
and the Great Panel at Altamira.

Sketch the hidden face in the air,
every soul that has ever lived.
One thousand with the job of remembering.

I tasted wild strawberries
and the realm of don't tread on me
and the noisome beauty,
and the Kingdom Hall air,
and I learned by looking,
and I copied the train moan,
and I rose up to Neptune
and went back inside the atom.

Share bread. Shelter and clothe.
The wound heals. The call is answered.

No false art, no fugitive feeling.

Holy forgiveness!—Ginsberg said.
Holy sonnets in a new year of grace and hope.
A holy thing Blake saw.
Holy antiphons. Holy lands. Holy Sylvias.
Holy Grails. Holy mothers. Holy Spectres.
Holy Joes.

Holy Cain and Abel. Holy Iago, prodigal son.
Holy Pilate. Holy caged birds. Holy the blind.
Holy the sweaty. Holy el.

Holy the voices of many heedless children at play
on the empty cornfield highway, shrill bliss.
Holy silence. Holy the despairing.
Holy the daughters and sons of despair.

And I heard the hiss of the sword
retempered in the new year of grace and hope—
the jungle-gym crossbar
arising from the cooling water, happy sigh.

        *

Holy Sinatra singer
in a cigar-smoke bar across from Carnegie Hall,
Laphroaig-drinkers and their women listening
and seeing visions and finding solace—
a bright, white altar cloth with
chalice gleam and bread amid
baby-sweet divine breath breeze.

And I hear on the bus
the unshaved carpenter's whispers
in a new year of grace and hope.
Faith yearns.

And I listen to the breathy words of
the line signed, the Confession and
the Creed, water-walking and
boils cured, jitters and baldness and
planter fasciitis and diaper rash and
evil cells, letters arranged in right order, and
the bright white hole of consecration.

    Let the little one de-code zero.
    Let the toddler lead the pilgrim company.

And I move my fingers
across the rough-cut altar stones,
hidden in a cluster of trees near Cricket Hill,
near the futbol pitches, and
across the lectionary tablets made from alabaster,
from marble, from the wood of an acacia tree, and
across the warp-woof of the galaxy of galaxies
beyond pain and fright, the raw wound,
above and beyond. The real thing. Do it.

Amen. Alleluia. Hosannah.

And I hear, reverenced, the water, the winds,
blood on its pathways,
night to day to night,
grave dust, quickening womb, embrace.
Embrace is reverenced.

And I see subdivisions of mercy in Kane County,
empty lots of tender affection in Englewood,
sun-gilded alley turds behind the Paulina two-flat,
more beautiful than lilies,
seven ways times seven, in daylight
and, of a night, in hard rain falling,
on the right hand and on the left,
before and behind,
end and beginning,
a new year of grace and hope.
Hazard no pride.

Dance, dance, dance.

From the shelves of the Rogers Park library,
I open books of empty pages, wondrous, and
in the ballot box in a Hyde Park alley, I find

the lost tribes and
the communion of saints and
the forgiveness of sins and the mundane chrism and
the catalytic converter thieves and
the tax-collectors and the porn performers and
the drunk and near-drunk and
an assortment of sinners,
me among them,
as if in a candy box.

Hear the joyful din. Truth endures to all generations.
A sign through all generations.

Blood and Flesh

You tell me to crawl
into the ragged slash
in your side and pull
the raw edges of flesh
together to enclose me
in the gory warmth of
your heartbeat, like
a babe at the breast,
like a love flesh to
flesh on damp sheets,
like reentering the womb,
like surrendering to the
formless white at the heart
of water, air, ore, sky,
plant, sun, star, cloud,
moon, blood and flesh.

Credo

I believe the witnesses of these things.

I believe the song not sung at Babylon riverside. I believe in don't cry, scream. You and your word. The history of a charcoal fire, fine fish and thick bread. I believe Hosanna, Alleluia, kudos, mazel tov, joy, transubstantiation, disputation, sorrow crows, notary publics. I believe in garments whiter than snow. Whirlwind blooming.

I believe in Western Avenue car dealerships, Halsted Street gay bars, Clark Street taquerias, storefront Madison Street churches, vast vacant South Side lots of buildings disappeared, labyrinth Lower Wacker Drive, South Water Market, Peanuts Park, Loretto Hospital, the gas bursting into air out of Bubbly Creek, the clots of high schoolers, dopey with youth, in McDonald's in mid-afternoon, the ostentatious simple of Daniel Burnham's grave, the painting of Msgr. Long posed as St. Edward in the circle high up in St. Martin de Porres Church, the pew there where the two who made me vowed to wed, the tunnel of el tracks along Lake Street that my 12-year-old brother, unlost, walked home seven miles to avoid asking for help. Who would answer?

Listen, I believe meniscus tear.

I believe the echo of the name-caller, the stained glass shattering, the crumbling of the eucharistic Saltine. I believe the red priest sermon, the baby's prayer for salvation. Peasant pugilism, I believe. Gospel cockfights. I believe I ask three times. The thunder out of White Mountain, out of the Church of the Holy Innocent, out of the Leamington gangway, the signboards weeds, the

Blacktop glass glitter in sunrise, the deaf girl who was my
playmate once, the aroma of incense rising to the darkness
in the ceiling of the apse. Walls shaken, my brother's
forlorn bullet. I believe lightning.

Want to know what I believe?
The yearn, turn, of the baby to light—the reach to hope.

I believe in the innocent knees of the thieves broken with
a sledgehammer to quicken the sag and strangulation and
death to fit the time parameters, for clergy convenience.
Together in Paradise this day. I believe in Mecca and
Saint Martin Luther and Saint Michelangelo, in Rome
and Saint Edith Wharton, Saint Chaucer, Saint Virginia
Woolf, in Buddha's tree and Saint Einstein, Saint Lincoln,
Saint Elizabeth I, in Jerusalem, Jerusalem, Jerusalem. In
Howl. In Song of Songs. In *Leaves of Grass*. In *King Lear*.
In Edmund's maidenliest star, the snow-white brow of
Moby Dick. I believe washed in the blood of the Lamb.

In the sunset light on the red brick wall across the street as
I awaited the cancer word—this, I believe. In the rain-snow
of my brother's final breaths before his trigger pull. In the
infant turning away from his mother. In the uniforms of the
father. This, and in the trunks of city street trees on the flat
grid endless from lake, north and south and west, miles upon
miles, squared, pavemented, urban fabric, sackcloth and satin.

I believe there is no God but God.

My belief is one and holy—erotic, anxious, competitive,
raw, unprotected. My conviction is my dance with death. I
believe in the fear of religion and the fear of the world, grit
and shit, the boundless beauty out of the corner of my eye, my

own scars, blood bruises. I await the spark of creation. I embrace suffering and bliss, jagged and smooth. I am, as are we all, innocent of power. I believe in the Book of Job, dung hill and all, and the bully-boy whirlwind who commands the morning and sends lightnings on their way. I believe in Ecclesiastes. Breath, mere breath, exhalation. In Elijah on his mountain face-to-face with a still, small voice. Cocks crowing.

My faith is the fingernail of a baby.

I believe the live coal the angel flew from the altar to touch my lips to sanctity.

How Puzzle the Prayer

Walking seminary fields,
silent-hour recollection days,
calloused caress of color and blaze,
sharp tender bright air slicing wet morning grass.

Filled with wide light.

How steel my legs?
How blade the grip lack?
How bell the jerk and jag of breath?

How pipe the foreign?
How altar the yearn?
How street the knowledge of death?

How ocean the benediction?
How rosary the examination?
How sculpture the confession?

I confess. I crucify. I abjure. I sacrifice.

Prophet's blood off rawed skin to splat road dust,
paste for blind eyes and full stomachs.
Blessed are the lost.

Lauds. Compline.
Psalm-song.
Psalm of David.
Psalm of the great empty white.

My God, my God, why?

How architecture the touch?

I will go to the table of the Lord.
Break my bread. Spill my wine. Wash my sins.
White my garments. Angel my innocent's neck.
Good news, good news.
Call me blessed.

How ghost the surrender?

Magnifying the Lord

In those days, I put the
braided cable wire over
my shoulder and pulled
the river through seminary
fields, through football
rectangles burned in
spring grass, through the
front road—no more
walking to Illinois Highway
1 in the half hour of free
time on the schedule after
supper before study hall—
through the speckled green
gymnasium linoleum, the
last place I saw George
before the aneurysm.

This day, I walk another
seminary road—a spy
in the House of the
Lord, unofficial, lone,
undocumented—past
bird feeders with white
crosses, past decorative
bridge crosses, speckled
with fuzzy efflorescence,
past the tall trunk, twice
my height, topped with a
rough wood cross, past
the sixty-seven-foot
column, topped with a
twelve-foot Immaculate
Conception Mary, her
halo stuck into her skull

with a steel spike, past
the red brick building
where my conference
center room has two
crucifixes, past young
smiling men of a
different rubric.

They are foreign to me,
even as they look like
George and me and all
the others half a century
ago, a time of worker
priests, social worker
priests, civilian priests,
ministering null souls
in null neighborhoods.

I ax the tree in a woods
along the lake, ax the
tree in front of the main
chapel, ax the tree in
my third-floor room—
the name of Right Reverend
P. W. Dunne brass-plaqued
on the door—where, in
those days, boys like me
puzzled God and enigmaed
Aquinas and breathed the
air of open windows and
depthed Psalms and Mary's
Magnificat. Timber!

I look out the window for
a pillar of cloud.

At this noon, Moses and
Aaron, Samuel and Isaiah
and Jeremiah are buried
here and there on the
grounds, the prophets
and archangels, saints and
martyrs, deep in black Illinois
dirt, mission fathers and
Monsignors and Cardinals—
Mundelein is in a crypt
behind the altar in the
main chapel—and I seed
myself in the soil, I burrow
in search of forgotten tunnels
to take me to something to
serve as home.

Young men in dressy
cassocks, young priests
in tight Roman collars
on this eve of ordination
weekend—I want you to
turn in your finery for an
air conditioner repair man's
shirt and worries, for a
waitress outfit for one
anxious job and a Walmart
vest for a second and kids
home alone, for the bloody
jeans on the body at the

front door of the drug store
and the shooters's car
keening away west on Devon.

I look out my window for
a holy mountain.

In the light of the
setting sun, I swallow
all the water in the
seminary lake. I am
Leviathan. I swallow
all the air, all the
sunlight. I speak now
from hiding. I swallow
mystery, body and blood.

I look out my window for
transfiguration.

I kneel for communion
before these cross-bearing
young men. I am open to
their rosaries, open to
their Stations of the Cross,
open to their wooded shrines
and devotionals, open even
to old anti-modern Pius X,
statued before the chapel
if these cross-bearing young
men learned from him
anything about how to
be a pastor. If he knew.

Pastor me.

I am open to their souls magnifying the Lord.

I kneel before them with my sacred heart in my bloodied hands. Pastor me. Jesus me. Bless me with holy oil like a baby, like a woman in labor.

O Anointed One

Show me the old town, anointed one.

Show me the kiva in the dusty old
pueblo where I cannot go up the
ladder and down the ladder to the fire.

I sweat secular sweat out here in the sun.
I know my place.

Show me the golf course on sacred
land, sold to buy other, more sacred
cliff and rock. The hotel, the casino
land, sold to buy holy lost dirt.

Let me walk past the pueblo clown as she
makes fun of me and distracts me from
reverenced pictographs. No fences
here, only the weight of belief.

Let me fail to notice the handprints on
the cave wall, high up, far above the floor of
the canyon. The mountain cat seeking shade.

In another place, I will sketch on
many pieces of paper a complex
belief system with maize at the
center for those who are people of corn.

Pilgrim

I journeyed the rocky shell of the planet,
ambled the upper mantle,
rubbernecked tectonic plates.
I was quaked and worked to stay in trim.
In moonless night,
a loon, insects, ripples on the water face.
Amen, amen.

Among the xenoliths,
foreign rocks of kimberlite and lamproite,
I moved across the skin of the stony sphere
—pulled as if by a magnet,
headed for home I never knew—
ending up in Africa's Horn, once called Punt,
God's Land. South of the Red Sea.
A place of plows, millet, iron tools,
mythic Christians and Islam
—patriarchs, presbyters, kings,
short-of-stature gods, aircraft deities.

Power was given
to two witnesses in sackcloth, prophesying
for one thousand two hundred and threescore days.

Two olive trees, two candlesticks, an iron rod.
Trail of tears.

The crucified one was
only a paragraph in the Procurator's biography.
The wife's dream.

And, now, here, with storming outside,
my household troubles with questions
of protocol and duty.

I am nothing if not dutiful.
Dutied to a fault.
In the bordered path of duty, I expect safety.

But the white lines of the crosswalk
are as an asphalt stain to the tires
that meet the road, kiss of speed,
barreling to deliver
through terror or accident or anger
two tons of metal
to ravage pedestrian flesh, break bones,
innocent as a gravestone, guilty as a gem.

I look both ways.

Foreheads Blazing

My pew at the Uptown McDonald's,
House of the Lord,
along the north window
looking out on the lace of
sun and shadow Foster Avenue
and the 146 bus idling in the cold
for its trip to the Loop,
Chicago Vatican.

At the foot of the black locust
rising like a saint from the sidewalk,
a broken twisted soul of a branch rests,
spiked and pricked,
neither here nor there,
no longer sapped and
not yet fired or landfilled.

The new day sun alchemies
the brick apartment building facades
into gold and art and incense
as, inside this sanctuary,
the choir is a wallpaper power ballad
—"(I Just) Died in Your Arms"—
a 1980s Sanctus, and, outside,
a sex angel, in pink mesh top
and deep bare navel and black bicycle pants,
dances and wiggles in a winter doorway,
filled, filled, filled,
and never a thought now
for the emptiness to come,
archangel of the new light.

The usher comes and offers me
a soiled Bears schedule but
I toss nothing into his basket. I
still have the towel a bag guy gave
me at another fast-food chapel. He
had enough to carry and nowhere
to rest his head.

He was transubstantiated
in our exchange and so was I.
Our communion was a moment
in our years of moments.

Here, now, the nave is filling with congregants,
our own upper room, and, every moment,
a pentecost, our foreheads blazing,
too bright for us to suffer or see
but we wish them there, yearning.

By trick of sun, I see myself in the plain-glass window,
among all of us saints and sinners,
as I stand to head to my Galilee
and Jerusalem
and Gethsemane.

This mundane service is ended and without end for ever.

Psalm Zero

Let me tell you:

Listen:

My father, self-statued
in every one of his
corners, joined me in
the upper room, and
my son, joyfully
tuxedoed—both tall,
both aching, both with
feet for me to wash.

And my brother, also
tall, washed white in
the 3 a.m. rain-snow
of the Lamb, his last
stains sacreding
cement and icy grass.

All named David.

None with the shepherd
king's song or swagger.

Lamentation

Let Israel now say,
let Aaron now say,
give thanks,
mercy endures,
mystery forever his majesty.

    Bulleted chaste gazelle,
    backyard cement,
    clot-blood hosed onto yellow winter grass.

I called upon,
put confidence in.

    Mountain defiled.
    Morning-dark body.

Compassed me about,
compassed me about,
compassed me about,
compassed me about like bees,
the fire of thorns,
raw flame and wild.

    Robes rent.
    Cup unpassed,
    drained.

My strength and song
not die,
gates of righteousness,
stone builders refused,
day dawn.

Bind the sacrifice with cords
at the horns of the altar.

> Devoid of speed and flight and fight.
> The finger squeeze.

Sacred holocaust,
the day the Lord has made.

Pray, a Sequence

—ONE—

Pray for us, wrong turns and potholes,
wildernesses, arbors, and roiled rivers.

Pray for us, Our Lady of Souls.
Pray for us, you, empty vessels and mute cymbals.

Echoes in dark,
pray for us, weak as we are.

Lady Cosmos, pray.
Timeless atom, pray.
Rotted wood.

Pray us trust.
Pray us faith, shadowed alley.
Pray us strength, isolate prairie tree.
Pray us father, son and spirit, footfall.

Rusted auto abandoned, pray.
Rusted crucifixes, pray.
Rusted shovel, pray.
Rusted furnace.

Pray for us, grassy knoll.
Pray for us, you, broken crutch and scorched milk,
shoe polish, Hosanna seed and neatsfoot oil.

Pray "Caution Falling Ice."
Pray "How to throw bricks."
Pray "Hose connection."
Pray "In God we trust."
Pray "No parking anytime."

Pray for us, soft steel.

Pray for us, fall-of-snow stillness.
Pray for us, now and again.
Let your prayers rise Lady Universe,
the incense of galaxies,
of black holes, of tick and tock.

Knife slice skin,
pray for us, numberless and miseried.

Pray blank paper.
Pray blue number tattoo.
Pray ignorant ocean.
Pray for us, you, stones and boulders,
jittering leaves, straight-line shadow and hot manure.

Bleak formlessness.
Thin humidity.
Blackened brick.
Tracked snow.
All that is hard and soft.
Wide horizon and canopy of heavens.

Beseech your Lady pray for us.
Plead your Lady.

Pray for us, Our Lady of Souls.
Pray for us, you, ashes and sands and black soils.

Mourning fields, pray for us.
Abattoir sewer, pray for us.
You, asteroid tails, give us prayers.

Let your prayers,
you, mountain face, water us.
Let you, stalagmite, pray for us,
and worn leather and ore slag, the whirl wind.

We entreat your prayers, Lady Creation.
We beseech in breathing and breathlessness.
We plead, you, minerals and geyser spouts.
Pray us, at nerve ends, hope.

Pray us, you, dust to dust.

—TWO—

My covenant with you,
with every living creature,
birds and animals, tame and wild,
fish.

My covenant with you,
never again destruction
by the waters of flood.

My covenant with you,
the arc of colors across the sky.
forever ages to come,
after clouds,
sunlight on water.

My covenant with you,
mother heartbeat,
fluid and waters,
ocean waters of Baptism.

My covenant with you,
relics lost in midden mounds,
broken oil vessels,
electric storm clarity.

My covenant with you,
dark sanctuary,
prostrate on marble, tonsured.

My covenant with you,
suffering breathing.

My covenant with you,
Huns at large,
bland Nazi memos,
slave blood on weather-grayed wood.

My covenant with you,
nature and nurture and will,
and the greatest of these is will,
the fog of selection.

My covenant with you,
spirit on waters,
deep monsters and monstrosities,
silence.

My covenant with you,
first step,
second step,
last step.

My covenant with you,
dazzlement, transfigurement,
delight, puzzlement.

My covenant with you,
ashes and boils,
toil, sweat and wonder.

My covenant with you,
song of sinner.

My covenant with you,
gold, stained-glass, soaring space,
beeswax and rubrics, incense,
pungent prayer

—THREE—

I was tempted to ignore my dust future.

I was tempted to vow.

Offered alms, I was tempted.

I was tempted to make a pass,
take a pass,
walk past,
pass over,
pass up the chance.

I was tempted to listen to the siren yowl
and orders for the taking.

I was tempted to run away to Disneyland.

I ate stones when tempted.

I was tempted to pluck out my eyes,
to sever my glands, to self-leper.

The empty room tempted me,
the parapet, the crowd of angels,
suburban snow-rain.

White gloves and a large-jewel ring
were my temptation,
the red cassock.

I was tempted
to pack up all my longings and forgiveness.

I was tempted to surrender
to the Whore of Bargain Basement,
to the Bishop of Phone,
to the King of Fears,
to America the Dutiful,
to the Garden of Heathens,
to Forever Young.

Who whispered freedom in my ear
tempted me.

Who looked in my eyes
tempted me.

Who bassinet-strapped me
tempted me.

I was tempted
to rock the boat until it sank.

My animal spirits tempted me.

The bully tempted me to feeling.

The pastor told me to avoid temptation
by picturing a naked woman defecating.

Temptation was my recompense.

Body and soul, I was tempted.

I was tempted to hope.

I was tempted by faith.

I was tempted to incandescence,
to phosphorescence,
to obsolescence,
to acquiescence,
to frankincense.

Atop the mountain, I was tempted.

In the ocean trench, I was tempted.

I was tempted
by the blank formless white.

I was tempted
by the melting crayon colors.

I tempted myself.

Alleluia

Light in the dark, loud rejoicing,
as at harvest, as at nuptials,
as when reapings are divided,
the yoke shattered,
the overseer's rod snapped
as on the day of freedom,
every weapon warped in the sacred flames—
the child born,
the babe
on whose shoulders
teeters a world.

Look, I Am Sending You

The archangel Michael

The archangel Michael stopped Friday
morning at the McDonald's on Western,
just north of Pratt, and sat hunched
over the corner table, eating his Egg
McMuffin and blazing with the glory of
the celestial throne and was of such
incandescence that local TV weather
forecasters announced it in ripe bulletins
—with maps—as if a small other sun had
landed next to the emptied and forlorn
Harley-Davidson salesroom, and floating
technicians up on the Shuttle looked
down from space to awe the bright spot
on the daylight continent, and the two
aisle sides in House and Senate adjourned
to the western steps to look out past
Ohio and Indiana to the southern end of
Lake Michigan where mere Chicago flared
like the Earth's great jewel. Love is
wide. And he was reading a book of
poetry in a language no longer spoken
and pondering his lacks and warts and
astral sins, knowing the need of penance,
and, pushing her foldable steel shopping
cart, the small woman, compact in her
oldness, saw his tears and offered him a
Kleenex from the box she carries in her
weathered leather purse and put a fierce
and gentle caress on his virgin hand for
a moment and smoothed the feathers
of his left wing as if he were a troubled
dog or a child shocked by a tumble, and
the surface of the earth opened and all
the dead of all time rose like a cacophonous

choir of random voices, random notes,
blending in beauty, and then, tenderly,
slowly, the rapturous radiance faded and
the wings vanished and the accountant at
the table was asleep, arms cradling head,
naïve body protecting his closed laptop,
silently a-hum, a-twitch, softly snoring
an austere dream of First Communion.

Poor Soul

Poor soul, old soul,
sign of the window.

Sign of lost soul,
track of lost tribe.

The woman's flowers bloom
six months after her sudden final week,
an explosion in the parkway,
a chaos of untrained beauty, unedged,
as the father with the two-week-old walks past,
his face gleaming like a Pentecost,
like these crowded, tumultuous blooms,
the baby a deep sea.

The priest here this holiday weekend
for the mission-appeal homily
preaches about evil terrorists on his island
—he says he uses "evil" instead of "bad words"—
heathens who behead, kidnap
—he was taken as a highschooler—
bomb the cathedral, shit before the tabernacle
and do "bad things" to women
to gain possession of place and people.
He has, year by year, numbers,
a spreadsheet of outrage.

The weight of numbers burden my dreams,
and gods disguised as beggars,
and the bone gate.

The greedy you will have with you always.

Pure greed, old greed,
the lost greed tribe,
roadmap to and fro in the desert.

Take this all of you. Take it. Take.

I greed a listener.
I greed an empty wet clay tablet
in which to embed my triangular script,
my EKG, my teeth, my big toe print.
I greed clay for a life mask.

The mission Sunday priest is rich in numbers.
Like a state senator,
like a candidate for the state senate,
hungry of power.
He layers them like an atrocity lasagna,
and the collection baskets are filled
with tens and twenties, loaves and fishes.

Behind the curtain, children
run down the halls of heaven
and tire and fall and cry and
are comforted.

Prophet's Chair

Under the ball of fears, a ball of hope,
no feathers, bounce, however inefficient.

The angel of the cornet comes
with the rest of the yard crew
with their noisy mowers and leaf blowers
and branch slicers. Soil stabbers. Seeders.

Melanchthon, Throckmorton, Saltalamacchia.
Swallow the raven whole, feathers and all.

The girl not yet three
sits in the prophet's chair until chased off,
lower lip quivering.
A spark, almost unseeable,
settles on the marble seat for the ceremony.

The wandering believer
reads his portion into sheer stillness.
The wise virgin has her lit lamp.

Elements of wine and bread.
At the ceiling of the apse,
decorated with Genesis scenes,
a child's balloon bumps softly.

Look, I am sending you.

An Act of God

She slept most of the day, skipped
classes, came out late afternoons for
a bowl of tomato soup as if the
kitchen table were an altar, and she
told me that the Egyptians boiled in
the foam of a roiling Red Sea,
choked as if on goat bones and
met wrath from the walls of waves.

And I said they were just grunts,
doing Pharoah's business.

She said Moses stuttered and Aaron
rolled his eyes and told him: "Take a
breath, little brother, no rush." His
hands were seared from wrestling
with the fiery branches, and his face
rippled with holy scars.

And I said what of all those
dead first-borns.

She put the salt side of the
cracker on her tongue,
a singular communion.

Transfiguration mountain

Come to where the sand begins.

Come here, to Madison Street
to the second floor flat over the bar
and its cockroaches and night noise
and the crude infant, lacking lines,
full of urge, graceless.

Come, stand on the mountain
and wait for the Lord to pass.
Not typhoon,
not earthquake,
not conflagration.
Scratch, itch, whisper, still small voice.

Come marching home.

Come, you who turn your heart backward.
Come into the cave of the patriarchs.
Come, trickster Elijah, coyote and raven.
Come, doubts and emptiness.

Come, herald the Messiah.

Come to stand hilltop in storm,
rail impotent at sledge rain,
wake to green morning and the fool.

Wake to green forest sighs,
stained-glass parables,
incense-enveloped tabernacle.

Wake in the place of old men,
place of blooms.

Come, the sharded pottery.
A cosmos of broken glass in dawn sun.
Feet of fog.
Come with the leaves of Eden's garden,
fragrance in cloak.
Come to the rivers in warpland,
deep Dust Bowl wells dry.

Come to the woman with abundant hair.

I am royal blue, lapis lazuli.
Bless me, Father.

The ship comes in.

Come Moabites, Ammonites, Edomites,
Sibonians and Hittites.

Jealous God, come.
Come, birth pangs of Savior.
Come, death rattle.

Title to come.

Hard times come again no more.

Come to my epiphany.
Come, I know not where.
Come, bandage the poor who suffer from disease.
Come to the dancing place by the river,
by water flow radiant.

Come, boy, to the altar of the Lord,
cassocked, surpliced,
a secret agent at the throne of heaven.

Canticle

Water-splashed forehead.
Product of times.
Cheek slapped, new name, chrism.
Child of century.
Sign of.

Communion of saints.
Myrrh burial.
Finger ringed.
Deathly afraid.
Rolling frenzy.

    Praying the uncertainties.
    Intoning the mysteries.
    Chanting the doubts.

Frankincense body.
All the days of my life.
Lips oiled.
Reliquary of gold.
Field lily.

Soil son. Sky daughter.
With you always.
Fodder.
Tonsure.
Kill the fatted.
Defend, do justice, deliver.
Derangement.

    Empty of urge for logic.

Wafer tongue.
Sin into words.
Breath into words.

Immutable trumpet whisper.
Wood sags like child resigned.
Great Wall. Great Amen.
Table of sinners.
Lift up your hearts.

Breathing.
Be.

Holy Spirit

Holy Spirit (in caps),
aka Holy Ghost, aka Paraclete.

With Father and Jesus = Trinity.

In art, dove,
like the one that left the ark,
came back with green twig,
like over the Jordan,
over the water over the Son.

The beloved's eyes in *Song of Songs*
were doves.
Before wolves, "innocent as doves."

Dove = peace.
Not eagle, warrior of the air.
No meek sparrow.

Aka Giver of Life, Breath of Life,
Wisdom and Understanding.

For Father, think Cosmos, all Nature,
Big Bang to atomic geography, overarching.

For Jesus, a guy you could meet.

Holy Spirit = sweet inspiration.

Dove = flight,
a flittering, ignoring gravity, riding breezes,
always whispering,
the still, small voice, the gentle breathing,
the soft itch of silence that Elijah heard.

Aka Comforter.

Dove = insight,
wonder of surprise.

Dove, sometimes called she.

Sunlight on snow: a history

What was the luckless ram seeking?
To get horn snagged in thistles, neck clutched
by stone-eyed Abraham,
stunt-manned, at messenger's command,
for terrified son at meeting of flint-edge and soft flesh.

From the depths of my dry well,
abandoned by brothers, I read the sky for odds,
unknowing my Egyptian bounty to come
and my famined brothers, bowed and bowing,
at my call and beck.

Three prophets aglow on Transfigure Mountain,
robes, sunlight on snow.

Three sinners:
Let us build three tents here and
this will be our home tomorrow and forever and
we will never leave and
we will glow ourselves, flesh freed, and
we will be as angels, as gods.

Get up. Time for home.

Jesus Meets Little Sister Sandy's Mother

He stopped on the sidewalk on
Leamington as the mother,
distracted on the fortress porch
in her apron, wiping her hands,
was getting the children into a line
1-2-3-4-5-6-7-8-9-10-11-12-13-14
for Easter Mass—there was Little
Sister Sandy, between number 11
and 13—and the mother heard
him say, "Love the one you're with."

The mother knew the line, had
poured over it the tasty honey of
ridicule, filing it with the joke word
"relationship," just lust, danger,
raw sensation and Beware!

She lived, the mother did, a Mondrian
life of right-angle lines but without
the red, blue or yellow. Black and
deepest nothing.

She gave no notice to the obese
janitor at the stairs foot or his love
advice until he offered, picked up
from the concrete, a silver key to
the treasure of breathing.

"No, thank you," the mother said.
"My door is well-locked."

Little Sister Sandy kept her eyes 1,000 miles away.

Adman Walked South

Adman walked south on Leviathan Boulevard
toward Brooklyn, announcing:

> *I will anthem sing tomorrow, prophet talk.*
> *I will speak in tongues.*

> *I will page poems, climb tree, sweep dirt,*
> *change rules.*

> *Draw the map,*
> *find the Savior, publish diligent voices.*
> *Hearken to the sound, scratch the itch.*

It was Manhattan so no one paid him mind.

He wore camo sweatpants
below a sharp white shirt
with a blue-pattern tie from his fraternity.

He dragged behind him on a leash
a black and white stuffed puppy, not large.

> *Rise up, set down, push away,*
> *elbow, head-butt, go, come, go,*
> *let my skin find the secret commandments.*

> *I will oath. I will shut. I will vex.*

> *Tomorrow, not today.*

He stopped in the McDonald's
near Avenue of the Saints
and took his Egg McMuffin up to the second floor,
empty except for a Bible study group.

He was sure they were praying for his soul.

He went over
and whispered into the ear of the young pastor,
fresh from his riverside jog:

> *I will bring frogs to the altar*
> *and unguents, oils from Arabia,*
> *first-born live stock*
> *for the gleaming blade.*
>
> *Interview the lost tribes.*
> *Survey the communion of saints.*
> *Answer aboriginal questions.*
> *Submit to interrogatories.*
>
> *Touch brass. Touch gold. Touch water-worn wood.*
>
> *I will open my mouth tomorrow to the rain.*

The paster continued without missing a beat,
"Turn your prayer books to Chapter 13."

And Adman left his table unbussed.

On the sidewalk outside, he opened his arms wide
—forcing several tourists from Chagrin Falls
to step into the street,
scrunching noses as if he smelled (he didn't)
and already composing texts back home—
and sang out:

> *Fire the newspaper. Fire the straw.*
> *Fire my infant photos.*

Walk the sidewalks bellowing, free or mad.

Grope. Grasp. Grip.

I will plant the sunflower.
Crush the rotten peach under my heel.
Spill the rotten milk on soil.
Step past the nest-fallen egg.
Intoxicate on grass mown aroma.

On that short Dutch street, Numbers Avenue,
Adman refused to look up
at the shrine towering over him
and all the other small beings
skittering the concrete lanes.
No romantic, he.

He was in the subway that day
and came up to the rain of bodies.

He has stored in his closet
all the clothes he wore that day.
still covered with gray dust.

He almost wore the outfit this day.

I will proverb tomorrow, psalm a lamentation.
I will flee down Chronicles Road.
Sightsee Transfiguration.
Circle the Black Stone.
Dine on the Mount.
Leave a footprint
on my brother's bloody backyard sidewalk.

Tomorrow I will roll the stone away.

Answer the bell.
Answer the phone.
Answer what is not asked.
You are going to answer for that.

Fire the wood idol.

I will tell the story of my life.

At the Bridge, he turns back.
He will not cross water.

He takes out his cellphone
and calls his dead mother.

I will fence land.
Carve soil.
Follow lines to their end.

Fire the evidence.

Observe the proprieties.
Provide the necessities.

Tomorrow I will be human.

My foot will step in the right direction.

She picks up as he finishes the message.

She tells him to straighten up
and fly right.

She tells him to hold that tiger.

The Bread Is Broken

Aaron

Aaron was his brother's mouthpiece.
Moses stuttered.

It was only with Aaron at his side
that Moses, at the risk of sharp death,
could order Pharaoh to let go the Hebrews.

Don't think Ben Hur.
Picture my sweet brother David
who, innocent that he was,
wrestled with his tongue and only to a draw.

David's death was ragged.
The Pharaohs of our world
—who seemed saints to those outside the family—
had harder hearts than
the one Moses and Aaron faced down.

I did not stay at David's side
but fled as far from Egypt as I could.

I left him alone before the throne.
He could get no words out of his mouth
to give him protection.
He was a lamb I left at the altar.

No angel came to stay his hand
when the weight of the Pharaohs,
dead but still alive in our sinews,
grew to be too much
and he had no words
to ask help
and he dragged himself
out the back door to
his death.

On the night of All Soul's Day.
I place your photograph, David,
on the table of the dead.

What can I say?
I can't puzzle words together to find you.
I survive. You do not.

You are an emptiness deep in me,
next to the emptiness those Pharaohs
carved out sixty-six years ago before you were born.

I fled. You stayed. You died.

Visions

I see the hand of God
write on the wall
the sins of the king.

I see the bloody knife.

I see the father
lead the son to slaughter.

I smell the burning bush.

I see the furnace,
three inside unburnt.

I hear the walls fall,
taste bitter herbs before travel,
stand on sacred ground,
see the salt woman, the honey and milk land,
the river red with blood.

I see the face of God.

I hear the Lord speak my name.

I feel the touch of fearful blessing.

Voices

After the cemetery, Job,
now childless, walked
alone away from his wife
with no place to hide from
the Lord as the basilica bells
tolled the hour and, across
the street, an army of souls
appeared in one hundred windows.

Job kept walking. On the
path, he met Mary, still in
her blood-dripped robes
from standing at the foot of
the tree.

Now, here is Isaac, the
look in his eye still from
when he watched the blade
near his throat. And, here, the
Maid who listened and burned.

And here, on a small prairie hill,
flaming with no regard for the
batters and clangs of the storm,
the tree that is the Lord.

Job climbs the tree and nests
in its fiery branches.

Red Sea

In this tempest, the
walls of water collapse
on my Egyptian head.

Not exactly an innocent
bystander. A G.I. in
the army of Pharoah.

I open my mouth to
drink my fate.

Babylon Dream

I dream of Babylon in this
Dunkin' Donuts on Addison
Street at Lincoln Avenue
as if each doughnut were a
golden brick that, one atop
another, would raise a tower
from which to look across
the wastes to the Promised
Land. By the Euphrates, the
bosses demanded spirituals,
but I give voice to the tiny
tune of a whispering God.
I hear secrets just below the
chatter of the radio that I
don't understand but want
to believe. By the Tigris, I
lived my exile but
knew my home was in a
garden not of my planting.

Testament, a Sequence

—The Good Shepherds—

Those shepherds smell
of lambs and the sweat
of the fields. Those
shepherds choose sheep
rather than us. They live
out in the wind and storm,
in the empty space that
scares any sensible soul.
What is there to grab onto?
They face the wolf and the
threat of a fall that breaks
a bone and strands a body
to its tick-tock end. Chasing
a lost lamb, they find the
burning bush and are scorched.
They are burnt and scarred
and talk to the Moon at night.
The stars are their sisters.

—Magi—

Three kings or wise
men or scholars or
rich men or scientists—
looking deep into the
warp and woof—find
an infant, as I did. One
wipes his butt. One
feeds him milk. One
tickles him and watches
the Cosmos in his eyes,
as I did.

—John the Cousin—

He leaves
the well-plowed rectangles of patchwork soil
for the mountain gap and the waste.

He puzzles the heat, emptiness, echoless expanse.

Crouched in the shade of a boulder,
he sings his life song.

Later, called John the Fool
by those who wear their fears like armor.

He thinks of himself as John the Lost.
He pours water over heads,
hoping he can follow the flow.

He seeks the delta and the sea.
He seeks the one above the deep.

—Zacchaeus—

Zacchaeus climbed
the tree to see. He
was a go-getter. A
sinner, gatherer of
taxes, putting the
squeeze on the propertied
and exacting his pound
of percentage. He
hosted the preacher at
a dinner and promised
not to squeeze so much.

Even to give back some
of his gotten gains. You
and I know Zacchaeus
sinned again, squeezed
again. Like us. Later, in
his backsliding, he
remembered the tree
and his edgy joy.

—Herod—

Pilate sent the Galilean to
Herod, a middle-manager if
there ever was one, and Herod
whooped in his delight that he
would get the prophet to work
him a miracle. But Jesus stayed
silent and wouldn't lift a finger
to bend a spoon or pull a leper
out of a wineskin. Herod and
his lackeys scoffed and jeered
without evoking a response. They
yukked it up, dressing the teacher
in a gorgeous coat of many colors
and sent him back on his path to
naked death on the tree, as Herod
took a nap and slept like a baby.

—Veronica—

Veronica wiped
the face of Jesus at
the side of the packed-

stone street the
condemned man
trudged with his cross
rubbing his shoulder
raw on his way to the
hill. He left behind the
image of his face on
the cloth, like the
Shroud of Turin but
no need for x-rays.
Did she hang it on
the wall of her home?
Store it in a drawer?
It was certainly an
odd miracle in
which no cure was
executed. Did Veronica
and Simon the cross
carrier meet later to
trade notes or maybe
just to look into each
other's stunned eyes
with no words to say—
then, interrupted in their
silent communion
by the angry cry of
a hungry baby, they
turn to see the
mother raise to
the infant mouth
her breast.

—The Arc—

It was efficient to
break the legs of the thieves
so their unsupported torsos
would slide down the wood
and cause their throats to
clutch for unobtainable air
until, in the course of things,
they were strangled
by the weight of their bodies,
a forced suicide.

The other was already dead.
His body was carried away.

Theirs, thrown into a ravine
to be pecked at by ugly talons and
gnawed at by dust insects and then
excreted in the nature of Nature.

I steal into this world and,
against my will,
get escorted out for
crashing the party.

I watch the scar-face
lift his sledgehammer
and measure the arc to my knees.

—At the Hill Tomb—

At the hill
tomb, she
finds nothing.
She tells the
guys, and they
run to find
folded blooded
linen. She sits
on the grass
of the garden,
and the gnarled
gardener is
there, his sweat
rich with grit-
clumped dirt, his
hair thisway
andthat. She
sees him take
the innocent
seed and thumb
it into the
maternal loam,
and the bread
is broken.

In Grief, Mary

The mother of Jesus
sets fire to the Seder table,
watches the flames eat the
cloth, shatter the wine cups,
consume the salt and matzah
and book, sunder the stoneware,
and turn the wood her husband
and son once planed to ashes.

She is Joan at the stake,
burned by the heretic fire,
God's empty vessel.

She is in the Temple, whip
swinging in her arm on the
backs of the coin counters,
righteous in anger, and
knowing now the coming of
the palm procession and
the reckoning.

Lowly

Save me.
Waters flood my soul.

In deep mire, unable to stand,
overflown by the dark waves.

Weary of woe, strangered by family,
aliened, unmothered.

Foolish, a sinner, sackclothed,
my miseries a proverb.

They speak against me.
I am the song of drunks.

In need. Sinking.
The pit is wide and deep.

In need of lovingkindness.
Hear me.

Full of heaviness, galled,
vinegared.

My habitation, desolate.
Tents ripped, ragged, wind-blown.

Bowed by righteousness.
Singing the demanded song.
Of seas and cities and every thing.

A coward,
as all, sinners and saints.

A child resigned.
Reach me.

All Prophets Are Failures

All prophets are failures.

All birds failures, having to land,
needing to land—
even with all the coasting
on gentle or brisk breezes,
calm interludes, even in storm—
having to, needing to land,
needing to, having to die.
Pigeon carcass on the snow.

Prophets die after failing.
They fall to gladslappers, backsliders,
unlisteners, stolid mudstickers.
Prophecy winds down. Limp spring.
The half-life of zealotry.
Alarm clock unwinds, bell-less.

Flight is temporary.
Gravity and grave reign.
Still, flight is required.

No one prophesies a fact list.
No one prophesies the dawn.

The prophet spasms his atom of truth,
spins it into the maelstrom of other atoms,
and sometimes it is a snow flake
onto a wet sewer grate,
and other times
critical mass
and explosion
and then pieces
to be picked up.
Still, prophecy is required.

Bomb is coherent.
Then, failed, it
powers instant chaos.

Bomb fails. Bird fails.
Prophet fails.

The coherence of failure
is the consistency of chaos.

Prophesy for Herod like a trained seal.
Prophesy like Daniel, like Joseph.
Unriddle the riddle until the next one.
Unenigma.

The Big Bang was a failure
and the cross and the Garden and creation.
Tree tempt. Entropy. Unheld center.
Darkness in the third hour.

The third day, an emptiness.

Ascend in flight.
Flames ascend over foreheads.
Foreheads fail.

Visions are faulty, murky.
Mysteries are failed logic.

True are dreams, empty of plot,
failures of storytelling.

Baby's breath is prophecy.
In the end, it fails.

The Boundless Perplexing Sea

Beatitude

Beatitude me.

    Ain't I meek enough?
    Ain't I griefed enough?

The point guard with the aching knees
picks up his dribble just before the three-point line
and preaches:

    Ain't I poor enough?
    Ain't I clean enough?

Tear tracks slice in harsh gym light
down his hardwood cheeks.

    Ain't I hungry enough?
    Ain't I persecuted enough?

The power forward yells, Amen!
I put my arms wide as if to fly.

    I will make peace.
    I am a child of God.
    I live in heaven's kingdom.
    I am in need of comfort.

The power forward yells, Pass the ball, Horace.
I cut to the key, rise and
transfigure the lofted ball through the rim.

Fifteen-thirteen.
We head up court.

Goddess

The Mexican goddess, wide
motherhood, and her children,
all girls under eight, alert to
the kiosk choices, and her thin
husband, studying the receipt and,
for no reason, remembering when
he was thinner, younger, and stood
waiting for work through the sun arc
and got an hour's worth at the end
and was paid a day's worth and
never got a chance to go back, and
he shows his vaccination card on his
phone to the McDonald's woman,
masked, who asks in Spanish, and so
does his oldest daughter on her own
phone, the other two too young to
need it, but the Buddha goddess
smiles, shy, and shakes her head no,
and the McDonald's woman gives her
a pass, seeing that it's nine degrees
outside and let's hope no city
inspector is around, not that guy
there writing notes on his receipt
about the thick stone idol, his mother,
weighing more than all the planets,
yet only a much notched shell around
a constant dread hurricane that
electricked through the soil and up,
like a dishonest bloom, into the
tendons of her many daughters and
sons, and the Quetzalcoatl goddess
heads outside to the car, holding,
with one hand, her coat half-closed
against the wind and, with the other,

her little daughter's hand and winter
cap with a cartoon animal face, the
sum of all joys and sorrows, and the
guy making notes, for no reason,
remembers the sun's morning shadows
across seminary fields when, younger,
thinner, he knew himself adrift on an
essential river moving away from
the interior and out to the mouth
of the boundless perplexing sea.

Hambone

One morning, Hambone John Doe steals into
the empty church well before the weekday
service and works his way into the stained
glass over the back pew of Jesus and the keys
and the guy called Rocky in Aramaic.

There he is, you can see him if you
know to look, just over the shoulder of the
one with the red halo.

Those are loaves of stone at the Lord's
temptation—another window—and Hambone
up on the tower balcony, looking down.

As the slant sun explodes the glass into
incandescence, Hambone is enfleshed in the
highway robbery victim, beaten, naked but for
a loin cloth, helped by the low Samaritan,
called names by the high elders walking past.

In windows along the north wall: Hambone is
the dead to life. The woman at the well. An
angel come to Mary. A weary shepherd.
Magdalene.

In this south wall glass, his is a righteous act.

Up high, he is there above the altar with its
gold steeple, taking his place inside Paul's
bishop's vestments and within his green halo.

And there, where the God is forming the planet
from mud and breathing his breath into the
mudball—Hambone in among the moon and stars.

Hambone in the tree of the knowledge of
good and evil, above the woman conversing
in the cipher language with the snake—
called Beelzebub, called Nehushtan, called
the Adversary—the man nodding his
lust for a taste.

Hambone as Mary in the rose window. As
Veronica with her Jesus portrait on a towel. As
the Judas body askew from the tree. Hambone as
the woman caught in adultery, called slut. As
the babe at the breast in the stable—called
Wonderful, Counsellor, the mighty God, the
Everlasting Father, the Prince of Peace. As
each and every sinner and saint, name no matter. As
each version of God, vision of God—bird, son,
father, mother, light from light, lamb, big bang,
atom iota, cosmos.

Hambone as every and each tree and celestial body and
fortified city and seder table and wedding feast. As
every inch of every square foot of stained glass, and
every casement, and every wall of this church, and
all of the land underneath this structure, and
all of the land there is, under air and ocean, and
all that is from always until forever—Hambone.

Song of Songs, a Sequence

—Break of Day—

I am sick with love.
I am the lily among thorns,
a bloom among the daughters.

Don't waken my lover until he is ready.
Let the morning linger on.
I will wait.

My lover is the apple tree.
I sit in his shade with great delight,
savoring his fruit.

In the banqueting house, above me his banner.

My lover skips along among the hills, leaps mountains.
A young stag, leaping, breathing deep.

My lover calls to me to come away.
The snows have melted.
The rains have cleansed the land.
The trees bud with bloom and sap.
The singing of the birds fills the morning,
and the turtle watches the waters.

He embraces me with his left hand under my head.
He is in secret places, hidden clefts in the rocks.

Come to me. Your voice is sweet above all things.
You feed me among the vines with tender grapes.

The day is breaking.

—Red Beauty—

Your red hair flows in the wind,
a race of horses across the hillside
face. Your eyes, home fires. Your
teeth, dawn's light. Your lips, the
line of sunset. Your words are music.

Tender oases are your temples. A
proud tower, your neck, the strength
of a mighty army. Your breasts, the
cheeks of a well-loved baby.

I burn frankincense at your altar, bring
myrrh for your balm. You are perfect,
without blemish, a beautiful line, a
nimble curve.

Flee with me, my love, to the top of
the mountains, to the peaks, to the
clouds, and we will survey our empire.

I am ravished in your glance,
breathless in your arms. I am drunk
on you. You are my milk and honey.

I live in your garden, one of your
blossoms, nurtured by your hands. You
are a fountain of living water, a song of
songs. The north wind. The spice in the
air. The tang on the wind. I read the flesh
of your scripture.

—Caress—

I seek you. My
soul thirsts for
you. My flesh
longs.

I have seen
you in the
garden. Your
lovingkindness
is the song of
my lips.

I lift up my
hands to you.
You are marrow
to me. You
are the fat of
the land. My
joyful lips sing
of you upon my
bed through
the night watches.

I live in the
shadow of your
wings. In the
caress of your
right hand.

—Wedding Song—

We exult at the joining of young lives.
We dance the dance of joy.

This is a time of merriment.
This is a time of wonder.
Who will argue at a time like this?
Who will find fault?

Fear is exiled. Jealousy is locked away.
We are in the land of milk and honey.
We are in a rich and fertile land.

We are anointed in these vows.
In these promises, we are blessed.
This rite is our consecration.
This joining is our union.

This is the time of the Spirit.
This is the time of bright visions.

Let us dance.
Let us sing our songs.
Let us smile and laugh together.

We are in the Promised Land.
We are on our soil.
We are where we belong.

Corpus Christi Honeymoon

Let us honeymoon
in the Texas town with the Latin name.
Let us hide out together
under the sacrament's cipher.

Let us head west into Texas and swing back
to wade in Gulf water, chary of jellyfish,
ugly as the thin plastic Walmart bag
in the branch of today's winter tree.

Let us jacket up in the early autumn cold,
not hot Florida, not Hawaii bright,
our own clouded place no one else would think of,
medieval as the vestments and the ceremony,
two coals burning incense clouds to the heavens,
abandoned pretty much to the harmony of us,
our transubstantiation of body and body.

Let us foreign ourselves for a week in limbo,
watching TV election returns,
a relative's midterm victory back home,
as if gazing from a pleasant Mars,
empty of going and doing,
capsuled, cocooned, changed and changing,
our own bread and wine.

Let us emerge today as we have each morning
since that vacant shoreside week,
together, to fresh surprise and communion.

Fare Well

At Ainslie and Clark,
he sees the clouds open
to the dark and sparkling of space,
back to the mass of energy in the beginning.

    Hear the call of the thunder.
    Cross to green forests.
    Hear the horn blow.
    Awake, you careless people.

He says: When my body lays down, bury me
in the soil, in the ocean, in the mountain snow.

Dust and ashes under the chariot wheel.
Funeral feast at Denny's.

    Fare well, fare well.

He hears the crows of suffering.
He keeps priestlike appointments.

In the Loop, he preaches
the gospel of thalmic matter,
brain matter, matter of fact,
nothing is the matter.

He kneels for the Pledge of Allegiance.
He kneels for the Holy Egg McMuffin.

Breath, mere breath.

He sees hawk flight, the footprint of his mother
in cement in front of Leamington—
a spasmodic gesture out of character,

as if possessed a moment,
a shout to the cosmos
from safe silent corner.

In the afternoon church cool,
the monstrance exposition,
bread and gold,
incensed.

He hears the Temple veil torn.

> All will be well,
> and all will be well,
> and every manner of thing will be well.

In new-turned soil in the median on Ashland,
he plants blank paper.

In her doorway, the sacristan is dead,
dining room table mounded with laundry,
the song's translation.

Spark.

Backup singers:

> Let the frogs rejoice,
> the dawn birds, the insect swarms,
> patterned noise, horde hum,
> swamped.

> Let the heel be lifted.
> (The awed one pilgrims her road.)
> Let the eyes be salved.

(The awed one pilgrims her road.)
Let hints of salvation snick at the edges.

A closed heart is a lost refrain.

Fire, fire.
Dry cold grit.

Colonnade Saints

Let me stand in the square at
St. Peter's so Mary of Alexandria,
celebrated sinner, can look down to
me from six stories up, from her
perch among the perching 140 saints
—she repented—along the top of
the Doric colonnade, sunlit and stony.

Let Nilamon the hermit reach down to
put his arm across my shoulder like my
dead brother and dead editor—the
anchorite who locked himself away to
dodge the bishopric someone wanted to
wrap around him like a perfumed prison.

Let me look up, shading my eyes from
morning sun, to the hymnwriter Ephraim,
his left arm full of a large book, his gaze
on the page as if startled as if by words aflame.

Let Spyridon look down on me with his
one good eye, the other lost to the
persecutor, and let him whisper in my
ear the secret of his survival of the
copper mine slave camp, death camp.

Let Mark up there keep looking to the
horizon for his brother Marcellian,
martyred with him but unstatued, as I
keep looking along every pavement,
parking lot and field for my brother who
unpersoned himself in snow-rain on a
dark November 3 a.m.

Let me shout up encouragement to
Fausta, removed from the saint book
for haziness, but still up here, ten-feet
tall, as full-bodied, unhazy, as any of
the other 139, a sinner like each of
them, like each of us, like me, and a
saint, too, even without the piece of paper.

Let Fausta shout encouragement to me.

Let Remigius convert me as he converted Clovis.

Let Marcellinus from sixty feet above befriend me
as he befriended Augustine and Jerome.

Let me look around me, across the
plaza, behind me and before me, at
the ten-foot-tall tongues of flame in
loud tourist t-shirts, brown nun habits,
halter tops, sun hats and diapers, and
let me embrace these painful flames of rapture.

Song of the swan

At the start, the leopard seal was formed
and the least weasel,
the raccoon, the stallion and all other creatures,
skeletons and skin.

Distances were set between celestial bodies,
speed and direction.
Rain fell.

Stone turned to dust.
Whirlwind battered the bloom.

Morning and evening, each day.

> Prophesy these bones, he said, dry with sand grit.
> Dine these bones, he said, and these sinews of stone.
>
> Cover yourself with noise, a shaking,
> with strong brass pieces at the wrists, ankles, neck.
> Stand like a cedar, legs like bars of iron.

I boast humble.
I magnify unashamed,
encamped on the righteous mountain, my wingspan.

I taste. I see. Hear:
The ears of young lions perk at the sound, hearken.

All my bones, none broken.

I Want to Teach Emma Who Is Two

I want to teach Emma who is two
to look out this window
at the chaos of yellow and green
on the mid-autumn tree
—not so chaotic when,
from the ground,
she can see the tree trunk,
solid thick, rising up and branching
and branching with myriad leaves,
each one a tiny branch
but bursting with surface
to feed on light and color
to signal the arc of its journey—
and to notice
how it looks now on this cloudy day
and yesterday in the joyful sun
and tomorrow with the rumble rain,
and to feel with her eyes
the touch of the grit
of the mortar and bricks
of the brown wall behind these leaves,
and to see with her spirit
the spirits moving around
behind that wall,
living the arcs of their journeys,
and to rise up
in her connection to mystery
to the heavens to look down
on this city, this world,
to look down
and see the billions of spirits
on sidewalks and forest paths,
on fields and in towers,

each yearning, each breathing,
each hoping amid the chaos of pain
in the arcs of their journeys,
to look down
and be one with those multitudes
—You, Emma, are multitudes—
and one with the world where they live,
the breathing, yearning earth,
as beautiful
as this mid-autumn tree
outside this window,
which is as beautiful
as every thing
in the Cosmos
and as she is.

Soaked

Soaked to the skin in psalms,
the hermit spends all day walking in city crowds,
a divine toy bounced and bounced again.

The storm of roses blizzards indifferent commuters,
unleveraged beauty.

At the table of sinners in a sidewalk bistro,
the tiny nun in heavy brown habit takes her seat with me
and whispers uncloistered fears and visions.

About the Author

Patrick T. Reardon, a three-time Pushcart Prize nominee, has authored fourteen books, including the poetry collections *Requiem for David* (Silver Birch), *Darkness on the Face of the Deep* (Kelsay Books), *The Lost Tribes* (Grey Book), and *Let the Baby Sleep* (In Case of Emergency Press). His memoir in prose poems *Puddin': The Autobiography of a Baby,* published by Third World Press with an introduction by Haki Madhubuti, has been described by *Mindbender Review of Books* as "the most improbable and intriguing personal account by a writer published in 2022, but quite possibly the most ingeniously imagined memoir by any writer in any given year." Reardon, author of the history *The Loop: The "L" Tracks That Shaped and Saved Chicago* (Southern Illinois University Press, 2020), was a *Chicago Tribune* reporter for 32 years. He has published essays and book reviews widely in such publications as the *Tribune, Chicago Sun-Times, Crain's Chicago Business, National Catholic Reporter, Chicago* magazine and *U.S. Catholic.* His poetry has appeared in *Rhino, Main Street Rag, America, After Hours, Autumn Sky, Burningword Literary Journal* and many others. His poem "Lent litany banquet" was a finalist in the 2022 chapbook contest of *Divot, a Journal of Poetry,* and his poem "The archangel Michael" was a finalist for the 2022 Mary Blinn Poetry Prize of After Hours Press. His website is patricktreardon.com.

www.ingramcontent.com/pod-product-compliance
Lightning Source LLC
Chambersburg PA
CBHW072201160426
43197CB00012B/2479